SLIGHTLY WORDS OF  OTHER FUNNY SAYINGS

SMILES OR LAUGHTER ARE REQUIRED WHILE READING THIS BOOK!

By
Michelle Jenkins

Slightly Twisted Words of Wisdom

Published by Montsho Publishers
Available in Ebook and Paperback

Paperback ISBN 978-0-9679795-2-6

DEDICATION

To my son Christian, better known as my little
surprise from GOD at forty.

TABLE OF CONTENTS

Introduction

If you stumbled upon this book looking for life lessons, useful knowledge or just simple principles you can follow to better yourself. Let me be clear. *THIS IS NOT IT!*

This book is just a way to put a smile on your face while giving a little wisdom with a slight twist to it.

Knowledge is Power

So don't tell people everything you know because they might use it against you one day.

Chapter 1: Beer

❖ Beer doesn't make you fat. It makes you lean; against walls, doors, toilets, etc.

❖ Beer: The breakfast of champions.

❖ There's too much blood in my alcohol system.

❖ Beer: The reason college students get up every morning.

❖ 24 beers in a case. 24 hours in day. Coincidence...I think not.

❖ They say beauty is in the eye of the beholder. I say beauty is in the eye of the beer holder.

❖ Of course I love you, now get me a beer.

❖ Beer, sex & drugs are a full time job.

❖ Sometimes too much to drink is not enough.

❖ Life is not a fairy tale. If you lose your shoe at night. You're probably drunk.

❖ Beer is the answer for everything even if you don't remember the question.

❖ Beer: Helping ugly people get laid since 1855.

❖ Beer: The only substitute for bacon.

❖ I don't always drink beer, but when I do...No wait I do always drink beer.

❖ To you it's a beer gut. To me, it's a protective cover for my rock hard abs.

❖ Alcohol is not in my vodkabulary but I looked it up on whiskeypedia and found out if you drink too much its likely tequilya.

Chapter 2: Cheating

- ❖ Cheaters never prosper unless they never get caught, then they might end up president.

- ❖ Victory is always possible. You just have to cheat to get it.

- ❖ Good things come to those that wait or steal to get it.

- ❖ Anything worth having is worth stealing.

- ❖ Anything worth fighting for is worth fighting dirty for.

❖ If I can't get what I want. I'll just take yours.

❖ Don't steal, the government hates competition.

❖ I'm not stealing my neighbors Wi-Fi. Their Wi-Fi is trespassing in my house.

❖ As a young child my mother told me I could be anyone I want to be. Turns out this is called Identity Theft.

❖ You stole my heart so I'm planning revenge. I'm going to take your last name.

❖ Honestly I didn't steal it, I just permanently borrowed it.

❖ Fear is a sneaky thief, stealing away precious moments of your life.

❖ It's okay to copy people to get by but you will always be one step behind them, so you better pick the right person.

Chapter 3: College

❖ Stay in school because quitters never win unless you're Bill Gates, Steve Jobs or Mark Zuckerberg...Wait, so you saying there's a chance?

❖ Plagiarism saves time. Just ask a teacher.

❖ They can send me to college but they can't make me learn.

❖ I graduated with honors from Anger Management school, so what the hell are you looking at?

❖ To steal ideas from one person is plagiarism. To steal from many is research.

❖ My college electives were sex, drugs and parties.

❖ Ignorance is curable. Stupidity is forever.

❖ College: Where showering is an elective and beer is a requirement.

❖ College is like looking both ways before you cross the street then getting hit by an airplane.

❖ College is like losing your mom in the grocery store for 4 years.

❖ Studying: The act of texting, eating, and watching television with an open textbook.

❖ Student loans: The gift that keeps on giving...bankruptcies, foreclosures, etc.

Chapter 4: Family

❖ Children are wonderful little tax deductions in disguise.

❖ Parents spend the first two years trying to teach their kids to walk and talk and the next sixteen to sit down and shut up.

❖ Children don't misquote they just say the things you didn't want them to repeat.

❖ They say you should never hit your child in anger but I'm not going to waste my happy mood to do it.

❖ Children will always brighten your day. They will never turn the lights out when they leave a room.

❖ Children are the penalty for having sex and not necessarily good sex.

❖ My kids think I'm an ATM, so I bought a t-shirt that says Insufficient Funds.

❖ Who are these children and why do they keep calling me mommy?

❖ Honestly I really do love kids, I just seem to break out in hives when they're around.

❖ The only use for a teenager is a tax deduction.

❖ I don't need kids, I married one.

❖ My kid beat up your honor roll student.

❖ My kid wants to be president. I told him to aim higher.

❖ I was put on this earth to embarrass my kids in front of their friends.

❖ My kid got your honor roll student pregnant.

❖ Your kid will never get on the honor roll unless the county jail is taking new students.

❖ If you think I'm bad wait until you meet my kids.

❖ My kids are so bad they have their own timeshare in hell.

❖ I always wanted kids until I met yours.

❖ Satan has to be in your family tree because your kids are bad as hell.

❖ Unattended children will be given an expresso and a free puppy.

❖ Happiness is living close enough to your mom to get a home cooked meal, but far enough away where she won't just drop by without calling.

❖ There were two meal choices in my mom's house. Take it or leave it.

❖ Cleaning your house while kids are around is like shoveling the walk while it's still snowing.

❖ Kids should be treated like animals. Push them out early and don't let them come back.

❖ If you want to teach your kids a lesson, promise them McDonalds then drive by 50 of them before you stop.

❖ The direct use of force is such a poor solution to any problem and is generally only employed by small children and large nations.

❖ Treat your children like hotels. Checkout time is 18.

Chapter 5: General

❖ Whoever said winning isn't everything has obviously never won anything.

❖ If you're only as old as you feel then some of us should be dead.

❖ Imperfections are only good when they're on somebody else.

❖ People don't suffer from insanity, they love every minute of it.

❖ Madness takes it tolls, please have exact change.

❖ Mental floss prevents moral decay.

❖ Budgeting is nothing but a methodical way of going broke.

❖ They say nobody is perfect but they haven't met me yet.

❖ By the time you can make ends meet, they move the damn ends.

❖ I don't hate people. I just...No I do hate people I can't even lie about that, at least not to your face.

❖ People think I'm going crazy. The jokes on them though. I went there years ago, fell in love and decided to stay.

❖ Friends may come and go but enemies seem to accumulate.

❖ I have seen the truth and it makes no sense.

❖ Don't make me mad. I'm running out of places to bury the bodies.

❖ I'm sorry you can't hear my middle finger over your freaking horn blowing.

❖ Sorry if I'm staring but I'm trying to imagine you with a personality.

❖ Keep honking idiot, I'm reloading.

❖ Lookout...I drive like an idiot, just like you.

❖ I tried seeing it your way but I can't get my head that far up my butt.

❖ No trespassing. Violators will be shot. Survivors will be shot again.

❖ One nation under GOD and under surveillance if you're on my property.

❖ I was addicted to the Hokey Pokey but I turned myself around.

❖ If you don't think anybody cares, stop paying your bills and see how many calls you get.

❖ Age is mind over matter. If you don't mind. It doesn't matter.

❖ Guns don't kill people, they just simplify the job for idiots.

❖ The voices told me you would say that.

❖ Horn broken. Watch for finger.

❖ I never forget a face but I'll make an exception for you.

❖ Start your day with a smile and get it over with.

❖ They say nothing is faster than the speed of light. I beg to differ, bad checks travel pretty fast.

❖ Old age is not so bad when you consider the alternative is death.

❖ A good friend is there when you need them. A great friend helps you bury the body.

❖ Stupidity is not a handicap, so please park your freaking car somewhere else.

❖ Everybody hates me because I'm paranoid.

❖ A clear conscience is usually the sign of a bad memory.

❖ Conserve water. Shower with a friend.

❖ Good friends don't let you do stupid thing. BEST friends don't let you do stupid things alone.

❖ Laughter is the best medicine and your face is the antidote.

❖ If you're following me, then you're lost too.

❖ Normal people worry me.

Chapter 6: Health

- ❖ Happiness is good health and a bad memory.

- ❖ Steroids are the athlete's version of hard work because college isn't for everybody.

- ❖ Vegetarians are not animal lovers, they're just plant haters.

- ❖ What goes up must come down, and if you're overweight you're falling faster.

- ❖ Steroids: The diet of choice for athletes.

- ❖ The secret to dieting is not eating more than you can lift.

❖ If nobody sees you eating it, the calories don't count.

❖ D.I.E.T: It stands for Did I Eat That?!

❖ Dear Diet,

Things are not going to work between us. It's not me, it's you. You're tasteless, boring and I can't stop cheating on you.

❖ Weight loss hotline. If you would like to lose half a pound right now please press one 20,000 times.

❖ Diet Plan: First step eat all the bad things in the house so there are no temptations.

❖ A balanced meal plan is drinking green sludge and going to the gym on some days and eating 20 tacos and drinking margaritas on the other days.

Chapter 7: Knowledge

❖ Everybody is entitled to an opinion, all of yours are just stupid.

❖ Two wrongs don't make a right but it sure can get you out of trouble.

❖ Practice makes perfect unless you're the next version of Microsoft Windows.

❖ Experience is what you get when you don't achieve your goal.

❖ Everybody is entitled to do something stupid every once in a while but some of us abuse the privileges.

❖ Sarcasm is the political way of telling people what you really think of them.

❖ If you don't think things can get any worse, you seriously lack imagination.

❖ People who think they know everything were put on earth to annoy those of us that really do.

❖ They say the early bird gets the worm but the second mouse gets the cheese.

❖ An expert knows a lot about a little but a wise man knows a little about a lot.

❖ Ambition is a poor excuse for not having the sense to be lazy.

❖ Indecision is the key to flexibility.

❖ The facts although interesting are generally irrelevant.

❖ Artificial intelligence is no match for natural stupidity.

❖ When I want your opinion I'll beat it out of you.

❖ I respect your opinion. I just don't want to hear it.

❖ I'm sorry, did it look like I cared for your opinion?

❖ Opinions are like buttholes and everybody has one.

❖ Everybody has a photographic memory. Some people are just out of film.

❖ A conclusion is simply the place a person got tired of thinking.

❖ Old people know everything, they just can't remember most of it.

❖ An expert is just a person that has made more mistakes in that field than anybody else.

❖ If sanity were dollars, I'd be bankrupt.

❖ Once I thought I was wrong but I made a mistake.

❖ If you make it idiot proof someone will just make a better idiot.

❖ I think therefore I'm overqualified.

❖ A synonym is a word used when you can't spell the other one.

❖ An expert is someone that takes something you already know and makes it sound confusing.

❖ 43% of all statistics are useless.

❖ Take my advice, I don't use it anyway.

❖ If at first you don't succeed. You better hope you're not skydiving.

❖ I may not be right but I'm never wrong.

❖ Be consistent, just not all the time.

❖ Admitting you're a butthole is the first step.

❖ Everything I know, I learned in prison.

❖ Tact is for people who aren't witty enough to be sarcastic.

❖ Therapy has taught me that it's all your fault.

Chapter 8: Life

❖ Change is inevitable, except from a vending machine.

❖ If life is a bowl of cherries can I get mine without the pits?

❖ Life is like a final exam, it's only hard if you can't see your neighbor's paper.

❖ Failure is only temporary, unless you're a born loser.

❖ They say the grass is always greener on the other side but all I see is dirt.

❖ If life is like a box of chocolates, I'm doomed, because I'm allergic.

❖ Happiness is living within walking distance of the local bar.

❖ I tried sniffing coke once but the ice cubes kept getting stuck in my nose.

❖ Death is life's way of telling you, you're fired.

❖ Life's a buffet, so bite me.

❖ All my life I wanted to be somebody. I guess I should have been more specific.

❖ The only time people compliment you on looking young is when they think you're old.

❖ Success always occurs in private. Failure occurs in full view.

Chapter 9: Men

❖ Behind every good man is a woman trying to grab his wallet.

❖ All men are good. Good for nothing or good for something.

❖ I'm the boss, just ask your wife.

❖ It takes a lot of balls to golf like I do.

❖ Wife and dog missing. Reward for dog.

❖ Remember my name, you'll be screaming it later.

❖ Men are only as good as their trainer.

❖ A man in love is incomplete until he's married, then he's finished.

❖ Everything that goes up must come down but there comes a time when not everything down will come up. That's when viagra will become your vitamin of choice.

❖ Men are like puppies. They are cute and cuddly but will shit on everything.

❖ Men are like cell phones. Just when things are going good, you lose your signal

❖ Men are like bananas. The older they get the less firm they are.

❖ Men are like computers. Hard to figure out and not enough memory.

❖ Men are like parking spots. All the good ones are taken.

❖ Men are like coffee. The best ones are rich and can keep you up all night.

❖ Men are like commercials. You can't believe a word they say.

❖ Men are like copiers. They are only good for reproduction.

❖ Men are like bike helmets. Handy in an emergency but otherwise look stupid.

❖ Men are like used cars. Both are easy to get but are cheap and unreliable.

❖ Men are like snowstorms. You never know when they're coming, how many inches you'll get and how long they'll last.

❖ Men are like vacations and weekends. They never seem to be long enough.

❖ Men are like insurance policies. They take too long to mature.

❖ Men are like high heels. They're easy to walk on once you get the hang of it.

❖ Men are like horoscopes. They always tell you what to do and are usually wrong.

❖ Men are like cement. After getting laid they take a long time to get hard.

❖ Mean are like a STD. Easy to catch and hard to get rid of.

❖ Men are like lawn mowers. You are usually pushing them around or riding them.

❖ Men are like lava lamps. Fun to look at but not too bright.

❖ Men are like makeup. They usually run when you cry.

❖ Men are like plungers. They spend most of their time in the bathroom.

❖ Men are like car keys. You can never find them when you need them.

❖ Men are like dogs. They will hump anything, anytime and anyplace.

❖ Men are like tile. If you lay it right the first time, you can walk all over it for the next twenty years.

❖ Men are like Chinese food. They're only temporary satisfaction.

❖ Men are like peanut M&M's. There's always a bad nut in the bunch.

❖ Men are like roses. You have to watch for the pricks.

❖ Men are like trees. You have to wait for them to grow up.

❖ Men are like bank accounts. Without money they don't draw interest.

Chapter 10: Money

❖ They say money is the root of all evil. It might be but it sure pays the bills.

❖ Money doesn't grow on trees because some of us would try to smoke it.

❖ Money can't buy happiness but it can get damn close.

❖ Absence makes the heart grow fonder unless they owe you money.

❖ They say you should marry for love. I say marry for money because it's easier.

❖ The best way to save money is to use someone else's.

❖ Borrow money from pessimists. They don't expect it back.

❖ Money talks and all mine says is goodbye.

❖ The quickest way to double your money is to fold it over and stick it back in your pocket.

❖ Poor is when you have too much month at the end of your money.

❖ If you want to make money from Facebook, log into your settings, deactivate your account and take your butt to work.

❖ They say that money doesn't bring you happiness. I say neither does being broke, so let me suffer with a new car.

❖ Need a friend, text me. Need a laugh, call me. Need money, you have reached a number that is no longer in service.

Chapter 11: Politics

❖ I know they say anything is possible but I didn't believe it until HE became president.

❖ If pro is the opposite of con, what is the opposite of progress....congress? Coincidence? I think not.

❖ If you can read this, you're not the president.

❖ Thank GOD we didn't have to run the 10 Commandments through congress.

❖ If we lie to the government it's a felony. If they lie to us it's politics.

❖ Politicians are like sperm. One in a million turn out to be an actual human being.

❖ The problem with political jokes is that they get elected.

❖ America was designed by geniuses, to be ran by idiots.

❖ A politician is a man that would lay down YOUR life for his country.

❖ Politicians are the same all over. They promise to build a bridge even where there is no water.

❖ If you repeat a lie long enough it becomes politics.

❖ If voting changed anything they would make it illegal.

❖ Politics is show business for ugly people.

❖ The best defense against bulls**t is vigilance. So if you smell something, say something.

❖ If you really want to see change, put the politicians on minimum wage.

Chapter 12: Religion

❖ God blessed everybody with something special. He just made it harder for some people to find.

❖ If you are heading in the wrong direction, remember, GOD allows U-turns.

❖ Going to church doesn't make you a Christian any more than standing in a kitchen makes you a chef.

❖ People the 10 commandments are not multiple choices!

❖ Jesus loves you but everybody else thinks you're a butthole.

❖ Church Parking Only. Violators will be baptized.

❖ Why pay for GPS? Jesus gives directions for free.

❖ Black holes are where GOD divided by zero.

❖ In GOD we trust. All others bring proof.

❖ The more you complain. The longer GOD makes you live.

❖ I don't believe in miracles. I depend on them.

❖ Don't make me come down there. Love God.

Chapter 13: Relationships

❖ I miss my wife but my aim is getting better.

❖ Marriage isn't a word. It's a sentence.

❖ If there is a soul mate for everybody, mine must have found out who I was and skipped town.

❖ If beauty is in the eye of the beholder, then some of us need glasses.

❖ There are very few woman that tell their age but there are just as few men that act theirs.

❖ It's better to have loved than to not have loved at all. Unless they took the house and car when they left.

❖ There is a thin line between love and hate. So take that line and strangle the person you hate.

❖ Time heals all wounds and a good divorce attorney makes it easier.

❖ Having a bad reputation is okay, it's only bad when you fail to live up to it.

❖ Temptation shouldn't be resisted because you may not get that chance again.

❖ They say sex is overrated but I haven't had enough to decide that yet.

❖ I'm through with love. Thank GOD there's still sex.

❖ Drink until she's cute but stop before the wedding.

❖ I'm not cheap but I am easy.

❖ The only way to get rid of temptation is to yield to it.

❖ It's okay to wake up grumpy but you better have her breakfast ready because she hates to get up for no reason.

❖ I got a gun for my wife. The best trade I ever made.

❖ Marriage is a three ring circus.
Engagement ring
Wedding ring
Suffering

❖ A bachelor is a selfish, undeserving guy, who cheated some woman out of a divorce.

❖ Instead of getting married again, just find a person you don't like and give them half of what you got.

❖ I never knew what happiness was until I got married, then it was too late.

❖ Bigamy is having one wife too many.
Monogamy is the same thing.

❖ All marriages are happy. It's living together afterwards that causes the problems.

❖ I haven't spoken to my wife in years. I thought interrupting her would be rude.

❖ My wife and I were happy for 25 years then we met each other.

❖ Terrorism is nothing compared to marriage.

❖ Marriage is a lottery but you can't tear up your ticket if you lose.

❖ They say marriage is about give and take. I just can't find anybody to take what I have to give.

❖ They say electronic banking is the fastest way to transfer funds. I say its marriage.

❖ Alimony is having to say you're sorry every month.

❖ Honey I understand the concept of cooking and cleaning just not how it pertains to me.

❖ Please don't tease me if you can't please me.

❖ How can I miss you when you won't leave me alone?

❖ Stop pretending you don't want me. It would save us both time.

Chapter 14: Tips

❖ Time waits for no one, so do all the dirt you can today because tomorrow is not promised.

❖ Never put all your eggs in one basket, especially if you're clumsy.

❖ If at first you don't succeed, destroy any evidence that you ever tried.

❖ When you reach the end of your rope, tie a knot and hang on for dear life.

❖ Always tell the truth because it's too hard to keep track of all those lies.

❖ Be true to your teeth and your teeth won't be false to you.

❖ When one door closes just go through somebody else's.

❖ If you can't find the elevator to success just take the stairs.

❖ If opportunity isn't knocking on your door, go to your neighbor's house.

❖ When life gives you lemons, make lemonade with a shot of vodka.

❖ Opportunity is missed by most people because it's usually disguised as hard work.

❖ Never count your eggs before they've hatched. You may get hungry along the way.

❖ When things go wrong find somebody to blame.

❖ Never go to bed mad, you're wasting a perfectly good argument.

❖ It's hard to look at the bright side of things if you're living in the dark.

❖ When the cat's away the mouse will play, so have a good divorce attorney on speed dial.

❖ Don't drink and park, accidents cause kids.

❖ Don't do tomorrow what you could do today, because today could be your last.

❖ If you can't convince them, confuse them.

❖ You don't have to brush all your teeth, just the ones you want to keep.

❖ Don't kick a man when he's down unless you're certain he won't get back up.

❖ The other line always moves faster until you get in it.

❖ If you find something you like, you better buy a lifetime supply because inevitably they will stop making it the next week.

❖ Never say oops. Always say Ahh...Interesting.

❖ Nothing is as easy as it looks. If it is, you're doing it wrong.

❖ If you don't like the news that's reported, go out and make your own.

❖ Always admit your errors before somebody else exaggerates them.

❖ You must learn from the mistakes of others because you can't possibly live long enough to make them all yourself.

❖ If plugging it in doesn't help try turning it on.

❖ When in doubt, just mumble. It still sounds intelligent.

❖ The sooner you fall behind, the more time you have to catch up.

Chapter 15: Women

- ❖ Women are like tollbooths. They always want money.

- ❖ Marriage is a woman's personnel Burger King. She will always have it her way.

- ❖ I know one day my prince will come but until then I live life one lottery ticket at a time.

- ❖ Pretty girls get everything and some of it's not curable.

- ❖ Size does matter even Goldilocks knew that.

❖ There's only two type of men, the one's I've had and the one's I'm going to get.

❖ Men, you can't live with them, and you can't bury them in the backyard without your neighbors noticing.

❖ Men are idiots and I married their king.

❖ I'm still hot at fifty, it just comes in flashes.

❖ Coffee, chocolate and men. Some things are just better rich.

❖ Whenever I find Mr. Right, my husband seems to run him off.

❖ I'm out of estrogen and I have a gun.

❖ Behind every great woman is a man checking out her butt.

❖ What do you mean I've overdrawn? I can't be because I still have checks.

❖ Giving birth is like taking your lower lip and pulling it over your head.

❖ They say not to marry beneath you but woman have no choice.

❖ The secret to staying young is eating healthy, exercising and lying about your age.

❖ Don't push it, I can go from zero to b*tch in 60 seconds.

❖ Well this day was a total waste of makeup.

❖ Get over yourself it's not as big as you think.

❖ I ran into my ex today. He should have looked both ways before crossing the street.

❖ A clean house is the sign of a wasted life.

❖ Tequila: Helping woman to lower their standards for years.

❖ All my problems begin with men.
   Mental breakdown
   Mental anxiety
   Menstrual cramps
   Menopause

❖ You say I'm a b*tch like it's a bad thing.

❖ Women are like movie rentals. After a few days you want to return them.

❖ Women are like fine wine. They get better with age.

❖ Women are like a box of chocolates. You never know what you're going to get.

❖ Women are like roller coasters. They're emotions are always up and down.

❖ Women are like the weather. They can't be predicted.

Chapter 16: Work

❖ Men - no shirt, no service. Women – no shirt, free drink.

❖ A computer is nothing but a way to speed up and automate errors.

❖ Our AIM is to keep this bathroom clean. Men your AIM will help, stand closer it's shorter than you think. Women remain seated for the entire performance.

❖ They say if you give a man a fish you have fed him for a day. If you teach him how to fish he will eat a lifetime. Work must be for people that don't know how to fish.

❖ Whoever said work is hard has never heard of workman's compensation.

❖ If train stations are where trains stop, and bus stations are where buses stop, then what are workstations?

❖ I can only handle one problem a day and today is not your day.

❖ There are 3 kinds of people. Those that can count and those that can't.

❖ They say to be the boss, you have to beat the boss. I say you just have to be a butthole.

❖ People that can smile when things go wrong usually have somebody they can blame it on.

❖ Teamwork means never having to take all the blame yourself.

❖ If you can stay calm in the middle of chaos, you probably don't understand the seriousness of the situation.

❖ Doctors are like gas prices, the more you need them, the higher their prices get.

❖ Children left unattended will be sold to the circus and you will be charged a service fee.

❖ Smarty Car Maintenance
½ hour $35.00
If you watch $50.00
If you help $75.00

❖ To keep our prison guards happy, beatings will occur every hour.

❖ Happy Car Wash. The best hand jobs in town

❖ Please don't throw your cigarette butts on the floor. The cockroaches are getting cancer.

❖ A bartender is just a pharmacist with a limited supply.

❖ Experience is being able to recognize a mistake when it happens.

❖ Advice is what you ask for when you already know the answer but wish you didn't.

❖ I couldn't fix your brakes, so I made your horn louder.

❖ They say hard work never hurt anybody but why take the chance?

❖ A cluttered desk heeds a cluttered mind but a clean desk heeds a cluttered drawer.

❖ Hard work pays off in the future. Laziness pays off right now.

❖ So much to do, so few people to do it for me.

❖ Sarcasm is just a free service I offer.

❖ I haven't had my coffee. Don't make me kill you.

❖ I didn't say it was your fault. I'm just saying I'm going to blame it on you.

❖ Amazingly enough I don't give a damn. I apologize for looking interested.

❖ I'd tell you to go to hell but I work there and I don't want to see you every day.

❖ If I offended you, then my job is done.

❖ I see dumb people every day at work, you just learn how to deal with it.

❖ We'll have none of that bullshit around here. It's bad enough I already have to put up with you idiots for eight hours.

Conclusion

So you made it through the book. I'm sure your IQ is tipping the scales now. I mean with all the great knowledge contained in this book, it would be impossible to not have improved a few numerical points right? Well I wouldn't suggest testing that theory.

On the serious side I do hope you enjoyed the book but it's probably best not to quote these gems to others, even if you are thinking it. Some things are just better left not said....I'll leave you with this nugget.

If you can't say anything nice, don't say anything at all and don't write it on Facebook either!

About The Author

MICHELLE D. JENKINS is the author of several books all available on Amazon. She lives in Rock Hill, SC with her husband and children. She loves reading and writing both fiction and non-fiction books. Michelle is also an avid traveler as new places and sceneries are a great way to get ideas for a book!

Other Books by MICHELLE D. JENKINS

THE CASE OF THE SKUNKED OUT BASH

A children's mystery book for ages 7 – 11. Join our ten year old detectives (Jerome, Mega Byte, Equation and Rock) as they begin their summer vacation. Who would have known they would get a case on the first day of their vacation?

UPCOMING TITLES:

- Got Smoothies? Smoothies for a Year!
- 104 Ways to Make EXTRA Income
- Simple Prayers for Everyday Life Situations

ONE LAST THING...

If you enjoyed this book or found it useful in any way I would appreciate if you could take the time to post a short review on Amazon. Your comments really do make a difference and I read all the reviews personally. It's the best way to make improvements for future additions of the book.

Thanks again for your support!